394
5.5

Withdrawn

FIESTA!

ETHIOPIA

GROLIER
EDUCATIONAL

Published 1999 by Grolier Educational
Sherman Turnpike, Danbury, Connecticut.
Copyright © 1999 Times Editions Pte Ltd. Singapore.

Set ISBN: 0-7172-9324-6
Volume ISBN: 0-7172-9330-0

CIP information available from the Library of Congress or the publisher

Brown Partworks Ltd.

Series Editor: Tessa Paul
Series Designer: Joyce Mason
Crafts devised and created by Susan Moxley
Music arrangements by Harry Boteler
Photographs by Bruce Mackie
Production: Alex Mackenzie
Stylists: Joyce Mason and Tessa Paul

For this volume:
Writers: Negash Debebe and Habte Lakew
Consultant: The Ethiopian Orthodox Church, London.
Editorial Assistants: Hannah Beardon and Paul Thompson

Printed in Italy

Adult supervision advised for all crafts and recipes,
particularly those involving sharp instruments and heat.

CONTENTS

ETHIOPIA:

Ethiopia is situated in eastern Africa. It is a landlocked country, bordered by Eritrea, Djibouti, Somalia, Kenya, and Sudan. It is mainly mountainous, with high plateaus.

▼**Addis Ababa**, the capital city of Ethiopia, was founded in 1887. It is a spacious city, where country-style dwellings and gleaming modern buildings stand side by side.

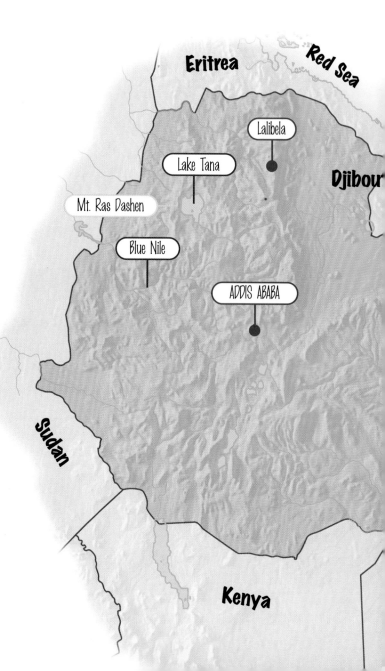

Eritrea

Red Sea

Lalibela

Lake Tana

Djibou[ti]

Mt. Ras Dashen

Blue Nile

ADDIS ABABA

Sudan

Kenya

First Impressions

- **Population** 54,938,000
- **Largest city** Addis Ababa with a population of 1,891,000
- **Longest river** Blue Nile
- **Highest mountain** Ras Dashen at 15,157 ft.
- **Exports** Coffee, hides, oil, seeds, pulses
- **Capital city** Addis Ababa
- **Political status** Republic
- **Climate** Varied, due to wide range of altitude; seasonal rains
- **Art and culture** Priceless painted manuscripts and twelfth-century churches carved out of the rock in the town of Lalibela.

▲**The obelisks at Axum** are among Ethiopia's most famous ancient monuments. This one is 60 feet high. It is deeply carved and represents a ten-story building.

Ethiopia

Wabi Shebele

Somalia

Indian Ocean

▲**Lake Abayata** and Lake Shala are both found in the heart of Ethiopia's Rift Valley. They are the favored feeding ground of thousands of flamingos and great white pelicans. These are just two of the 150 species of bird that visit the lakes; others include herons, storks, and ibises.

RELIGIONS

For almost 1,600 years Christianity and one royal family guided Ethiopians. Society changed very little over the centuries. A civil war in 1974 almost destroyed this old culture but not its faith.

ETHIOPIA claims to be the oldest Christian country in the world but its history goes back long before it accepted this faith. Nine hundred years before the birth of Christ the people learned the Laws of Moses, and the Old Testament was the basis for their faith. These laws are followed by those of the Jewish faith. The laws were brought to the country by the Queen of Sheba. It is said her son was the first of the family who reigned over Ethiopia until 1974.

About 300 years after the birth of Christ Ethiopia was converted to Christianity. The Ethiopian Orthodox Church grew from the early church based in Constantinople, now the city of Istanbul in Turkey. Over the centuries the remote, mountain people of Ethiopia have retained the artistic style and mystical services of the early Christian church. In this way it is very like the Orthodox and Eastern Churches of Egypt, Syria, Greece, and Armenia.

About A.D. 800 the Islamic faith became a force in northern Africa and found a number of converts in Ethiopia. However, the Ethiopian Orthodox Church continued to hold its strong national position through its close ties to the royal family.

In 1974 a civil war broke out in Ethiopia. The king, Haile Selassie, was forced to leave his country. Military men who did not like the church came to power. The war is over, but the royal family has not been allowed to return to Ethiopia.

GREETINGS FROM **ETHIOPIA**

There are about 70 different ethnic groups in Ethiopia. They speak different languages and follow either the Christian or Muslim religion. There are many different spoken languages, but the three main languages are Amharic, Tigrigna, and Oromo. The official language is Amharic. The Amharic alphabet is derived from *Geez* and *Ethiopic* writing.

   The Ethiopians also have a 13-month calendar. The last month is only 5 days long, and the other 12 months are 30 days each. The new year is celebrated in the first week of September.

How do you say...

Hello
   Tena-yist-illin

How are you?
   Tena-yisti-illin?

My name is...
   Sime ... naw

Goodbye
   Dhana hunu

Thank you
   Ameseginaleu

Peace
   Selam

7

ENKUTATASH

*On September 14 the **Enkutatash** festival celebrates the spring and a new year. This day, however, marks more than a change in seasons. It has historic importance, too.*

This new year celebration combines three elements in the civilization of Ethiopia.

The first concerns history. About 900 years before the birth of Christ the Queen of Sheba went to visit King Solomon in Jerusalem. She came home in September and gave birth to Menelik, the first true king of Ethiopia.

This king and his descendants – his family who came after him – ruled Ethiopia until 1974. Then a civil war in the country drove away the royal family.

When the Queen of Sheba returned from Jerusalem all those years ago, her officials welcomed her home with rich jewels. Those presents are remembered in the word *Enkutatash*. It means "Jewels to take care of your needs." It has a second meaning, too: "Diamond rings for your fingers."

The Queen of Sheba came home to what

The coffee ritual is an important part of Enkutatash. The carefully selected beans wait in a basket tray. Then they are ground by hand before the coffee is prepared in the pot. It is a slow process and brings a calm, welcome break in the festivities.

is now Ethiopia in September. This month marks the end of the dreary, rainy season and the start of spring. So Enkutatash celebrates the farming year. This pleases the Ethiopians because most are farmers.

This heavy candlestick can hold a thick candle that burns slowly. These candles are designed to last throughout long church services.

Oh flowers, have you seen them, in full bloom, in full bloom.
Come in one by one my dear friends
Till the wood I hew down shall build my own house.
Repeat chorus.

ENKUTATASH

A - be - ba a - ye - hu Lemi - lem A - be - ba a - ye - hu Lemi - lem

Ba - len - jer - o - chi - e Lemi - lem Ku -
En - qua - nis - be - it Lemi - lem A -

mu — be - te - ra Lemi - lem En - chet — seb - ir - ei
tir — ye - le - ni Lemi - lem Ke - de - ji a - dira - lehu

Lemi - lem Be - it is - ki - se - ra Lemi - lem
Lemi - lem Ko - - keb si - ko tir Lemi - lem

A - be - ba! — Be - en - ku - ta - tash e - lil e - lil e - ni - bel

9

China cups are available in modern Ethiopia, but many still prefer the old mugs carved of horn.

The third element of this festival is the honoring of the saint, John the Baptist. This saint's life was so pure and holy Jesus went to him to be baptized.

On the eve of the Enkutatash festival the priests show their respect for Saint John by praying, singing, and dancing all night.

People start the festival day with ritual bathings in nearby springs or rivers. This act symbolizes a fresh start to the new year. As they bathe, people recite a short prayer asking for a happy and good future.

All the houses, too, are cleaned. They are perfumed with myrrh, a sweet-smelling gum taken from a local tree. Fresh straw and little daisies are strewn across the floors.

A festive meal is prepared. Beef stews, spicy chicken stews, and lamb are served on plate-sized circles of fried bread dough. Friends and family share the meal. Gifts and good wishes are exchanged.

Every new year the grownups expect a certain gift from the little girls, who rush off in the morning to pick

Spring in the highlands of Ethiopia is a beautiful season of clear blue skies and acres of wild flowers. Religious art, jewelry, and household decorations copy the beauty of this natural world. Birds and flowers are favorite themes.

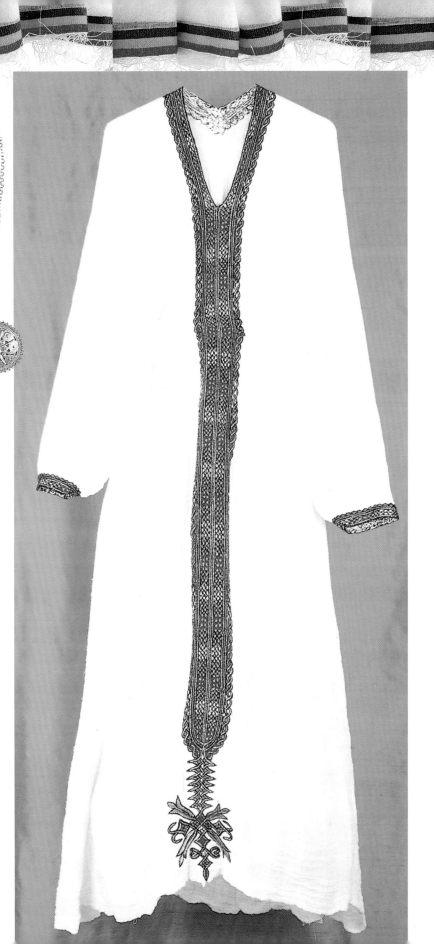

Everything is fresh to greet the new year. New or special clothes may be worn. Gifts of jewelry echo the gifts the Queen of Sheba received from her court officials.

little bunches of daisies from the fields. They go around their neighborhood with these small bouquets, offering them to the adults. They beat a small drum and sing as they go from door to door.

The boys paint watercolor scenes of the saints surrounded by flowers. They give these to family and friends who visit.

The little girls and boys are given money and other kinds of gifts in return for the paintings and flowers they have given to all the adults.

THE QUEEN OF SHEBA

Nine hundred years before Christ the Queen of Sheba met Solomon, king of the Israelites. Their son became a king and brought a great gift to his land.

MAKEDA, QUEEN OF SHEBA ruled over great lands in Africa. On the modern map these countries are Ethiopia and Yemen. Travelers came to her palace in Sabea, now called Axum, in Ethiopia. They told her of an even mightier monarch, King Solomon, who ruled the Israelites.

Makeda listened to the stories about the beautiful palaces and great wealth of Solomon. She was told he was wise and good. Makeda decided to visit Solomon. A great caravan of camels and men was prepared for her journey. The animals were loaded with gold, spices, and semi-precious stones. Makeda rode in splendor on the fastest camel.

King Solomon was delighted with his beautiful visitor. Makeda learned for herself the kindness and deep wisdom of Solomon. The king begged her to stay with him. Makeda replied that he was not to force her to do anything. The king told her that if she accepted anything from him, she would be obliged to stay with him. The two laughed happily at this bargain.

Late that night Makeda woke and felt very thirsty. She called to the king's servants to bring her water. Solomon was delighted. The queen of Sheba had accepted a cup of water from him, and now she must meet her part of the bargain.

Makeda stayed with Solomon. She studied the faith and the laws of the Israelites, who are known as Jews in the modern world. She gave Solomon a son, Menelik.

Eventually, the queen and her son returned to their own land. When he was grown up, Menelik returned to Jerusalem. He found the Ark of the Covenant, the tablets on which God Himself wrote the Ten Commandments. Menelik took the Ark to Ethiopia. His people called it the *Tabot* and hid it in the church in Axum. It has stayed there, safe and sound, for nearly 3,000 years.

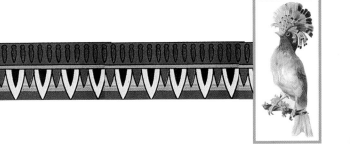

TIMKET

This popular religious festival celebrates Christ's baptism. It also honors the archangel Saint Michael, who has always cared for and guarded Ethiopia.

Before Jesus started His life's work of teaching, He stepped into water as a symbolic act to wash away all sins. This act, called baptism, is now a Christian ritual. A prophet, called John the Baptist, helped Jesus when He went into the River Jordan.

Timket is a celebration of Jesus Christ's baptism, and festivities last for three days. The first day is called *Ketera*. On January 19 church groups gather to select a river or pool to symbolize the River Jordan.

The priests, in very solemn mood, collect their precious *Tabots* from their churches. The Tabot is a tablet of stone or wood, or it may be a scroll. It has the

The skin of this drum has a painting of people cooking over a fire. This is a fine image for Ketera, when especially good meals are eaten.

Ten Commandments written upon it. On Ketera the Tabot is first wrapped in fine cloth and then carried on the head of a priest. Other priests carry censers of incense, elaborate crosses, and colorful umbrellas. Sunday school choirs follow, singing and beating a drum, the *kebero*. Everybody crowds around, but they let war veterans take a front row.

The procession stops to collect the priests and faithful from other churches. On arrival near the water the Tabots are placed in special tents. Everyone then gathers around to sing prayers throughout the night. They pray to make the water holy and fit for the ritual of baptism. They stop at dawn.

People dip into the water, or it is sprinkled over them by a bishop. Then the Tabots are carried back to the churches, except for one, the Tabot of the archangel Michael.

The following day, the third day of the festival, is the feast day for this saint and everyone gathers in the fields near the baptismal water. All are dressed in their best. They eat lamb casseroles or spicy chicken stews. The day is given over to singing and dancing. Teams of horse riders hold races that are cheered noisily by rival spectators.

Girls in Ethiopia are kept at home and only go out with their family. Traditionally, this is the day when they are allowed to meet young men, fall in love, and make plans to marry.

The singing is led by choir masters and doctors of music. The instrument here is a kerra, *and the one on the opposite page is a* masinko. *The priests' umbrellas shield the Tabots from the sun.*

SAINT JOHN THE BAPTIST

John brought an important message to his world about the coming of Jesus. He spoke out about the wrongs around him and paid for it with his life.

JOHN THE BAPTIST was the son of Elizabeth and Zechariah. His birth came as a surprise to the elderly couple. They had always wanted a baby but, disappointed, had resigned themselves to being childless.

They were told of the child's coming birth by the archangel Gabriel. He appeared to Zechariah, a humble priest, in the Temple. He was told that John was to be God's messenger and would tell the world of the coming of Jesus.

John was brought up in humble circumstances. Later he went to live alone in the desert. He survived on locusts and wild honey and wore clothes made of camels' hair. It was during this time that God's purpose was revealed to him.

John began to preach and to teach. He was such a powerful speaker that crowds were drawn to this strange and wild-looking man. John was very outspoken. He told the people that they were doing wrong. Those who wanted to live better lives were baptized by him in the River Jordan. This was a sign that their sins were washed away.

One day Jesus came to see John. They were related – their mothers were cousins – but they had never met. John immediately recognized

Jesus as the king promised by God. He felt very humble and was surprised when Jesus asked him to baptize him. As Jesus came out of the water, a dove appeared above him, and a voice was heard to say, "Thou art my beloved Son, in whom I am well pleased."

John grew in popularity, but he earned the hatred of King Herod Antipas. He had divorced his wife in order to marry Herodias, the wife of his half-brother. This was wrong under Jewish law. John confronted the king and was flung into prison. Herod's new wife hated John and wanted him dead. She found her chance during her husband's birthday party. When her daughter Salome danced to entertain the guests, Herod was so entranced that he promised her anything she wanted. Prompted by her mother, Salome demanded the head of John the Baptist.

Maskel

Over 1,000 years ago a holy woman found the remains of Jesus's cross. On September 14 her discovery is celebrated with bonfires and horseraces.

Maskel recalls the drama of Helena, empress of Rome, who was born in A.D. 248. Three hundred and twenty-six years after the crucifixion of Christ she found the cross on which He was hung. She had spent many years in her search for the "true cross." At last a wise old man told her to light a fire. He said she must follow the direction of the smoke. In this way she found the cross.

Every year huge piles of wood and

Priests carry fly whisks made of horse hair. Ethiopian artists create lovely variations of the cross, the symbol of Christianity. Many are displayed in the Maskel procession.

twigs are built for Maskel. The wood symbolizes the cross. Each village builds its pile, and each family adds its own bundle of twigs called a *chebo*. The bonfire, or *Maskel Demera*, grows huge. Some families prefer to keep their chebos at home. They burn them on Maskel.

Maskel starts with the arrival of the priests. All are dressed in rich robes and hold beautiful ceremonial crosses. Many colorful priestly umbrellas are also held aloft. The faithful crowd round.

The priests chant prayers of blessing on the Maskel Demara. These are followed by the singing of sacred hymns. Finally, the most respected person among the elders of the community has the honor of lighting the blessed bonfire. It is a special moment in the festival.

THE TRUE CROSS

Saint Helena, the empress, believed she found the cross of Jesus in a cave near the site of His crucifixion. It was kept as a treasured reliquary in Jerusalem. A reliquary is a sacred relic. However, it was taken from the city during a war in A.D. 614. After another battle, in A.D. 628, it was returned to Jerusalem. For centuries after Helena's find Christians looked for fragments of the "true cross." Pilgrims went to Jerusalem to find pieces. Beautiful boxes were made to keep the splinters. Churches kept their reliquaries in a shrine. To own a bit of the cross was to be blessed.

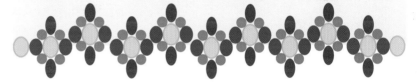

The people stand around the burning bonfire and sing to welcome spring, the "the season of flowers." Many take ash from the fire to draw a cross on their foreheads. They believe the ash heals illness. Feasting, dancing, and singing mark the end of the Maskel festivities.

The horseraces start after the fire. The animals are dressed in fine fabrics and colorful harnesses. The crowds are very noisy when they cheer for their favorite horse to win.

MAKE AN "ETHIOPIAN" CROSS

Ethiopian crosses are usually made of metal or wood. They are decorated with intricate markings. Make your own cross using plaster and silver paint.

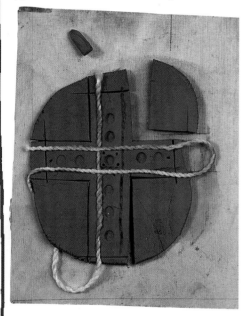

1 Roll modeling clay onto a flat surface so that it makes a circle roughly 6" in circumference and about ¼" thick. Use a pencil to mark a cross in the clay. Scratch a design on the cross. Cut the cross shape by pulling taut string through the clay, or use a kitchen knife.

2 Roll more clay to cut into strips each about ½" in width. Use these strips to build a wall around the cross. Smooth the edges of the cross and wall firmly together, particularly at the corners. Make a small cylinder of clay about ½" long. Put it about ¼" from the top of the upright length of the cross (in the center). This will make a hole so that the cross can be threaded and hung from your neck.

YOU WILL NEED
Rolling pin
Modeling clay
Pencil
String
Plaster
3 yards of wool yarn
Silver paint
Paint brush

3 While the clay is still wet, mix the plaster according to the instructions and pour it into your cross. The illustration shows that the cylinder of clay is not covered by plaster. If plaster leaks, quickly press some clay into the gap. Leave the plaster for several hours to set and dry. Peel off the clay mold. Paint the whole cross with the silver paint.

4 To hang the cross, cut three pieces of yarn, each about 36" long. Braid them and loop the braid through the hole in the cross. Pass the two ends through the loop. Tie the ends together.

FASIKA

The faithful go without meat and pray long hours as they wait for **Fasika,** *that is, Easter. Afterward they enjoy a festive meal.*

Fasika is a serious event. It is also called *Fasika-Tenssaie.* The word *Tenssaie* means "Resurrection."

Most Christians fast for the 40 days of Lent before Easter. The fast recalls Christ's suffering. In Ethiopia the fasting lasts for 55 days. The people of Ethiopia honor the suffering of the prophet Moses as well as Jesus's pain. During this time of Lent, called *Hudade,* nobody eats meat or any dairy products.

For three hours every day the faithful go to Mass, where they listen to sad songs called *Begena.* These are played on ten-stringed harps.

One week before Fasika the mood lightens. On Palm Sunday, called *Hosanna,* the people carry tall palm leaves and crosses to recall Christ's very last journey into Jerusalem, when cheering crowds cleared His path with palm branches.

After Hosanna is *Semune himamat,* or

The people go without meat or milk to honor Christ's suffering. However, on the day of His resurrection they enjoy a feast. Large woven tables are laden with Fasika meals of lamb, beef, or chicken. These are served with beers called tela *and* tej.

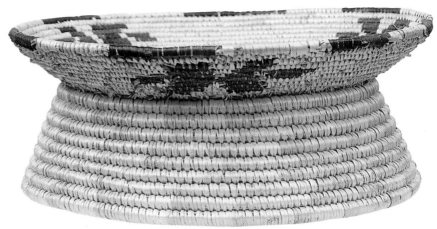

Passion Week, Christ's last week on Earth. The faithful eat nothing for the three days Christ was crucified, died, and was buried.

Sunday marks the day Christ came alive again. He was resurrected. The long night Mass ends as the dawn opens to a day of joy.

During Hudade priests and the faithful eat once a day. The meal is of lentils and vegetables, but not meat. Hours are spent thinking on the crucifixion and praying before symbolic crosses.

LENTIL STEW

Pour the lentils into a sieve, then rinse well and drain. Pick through them and discard any small stones or twigs you find. Put them in a large pot, add water to cover, and boil for 10 minutes.

Put the oil, garlic, ginger, and chopped onions into a large pan and cook until they are soft, stirring frequently. Add the salt, spices, and tomatoes. Stir to mix.

Add the lentils and their liquid and mix well. Cover and simmer for 40 minutes, until the lentils are very soft.

TO SERVE 8
1 lb. red lentils
2 T. oil
3 onions, chopped
1 t. chopped garlic
½ t. cardamom
½ t. cumin
½ t. coriander
1 t. salt
2 cups canned tomatoes

KULUBI GABRIEL

Thousands of people travel twice yearly to a small town called Kulubi. There they pray for favors from Saint Gabriel. These pilgrimages have come to be called "Kulubi Gabriel."

Archangel Gabriel is the patron saint of the country. Festivals are held in his name twice a year. There is a church named after the saint in the little town of Kulubi in eastern Ethiopia. On July 26 and December 28 thousands of pilgrims gather in Kulubi.

The Christians of Ethiopia believe that Saint Gabriel performs miracles within this church. Believers come to this shrine with prayers to cure illness, bring happiness to their family, or to give them a baby. About 300,000 people make their annual pilgrimage to Kulubi from all parts of the country.

Many bring votive offerings, that is, gifts to support their pleas for a miracle. They offer crosses, carpets, rings, candles, incense, and umbrellas. These gifts are put in a deep, wide hole. Cattle are also herded to Kulubi as votive offerings – but they are not put in the big hole!

The people who have had their wishes granted by the saint also attend the festival. To show their grati-

Candles play a big role in church ritual. Pilgrims make gifts of candles to the saint. They carry these gifts in round leather bags.

tude, some walk barefoot for 30 miles. Others crawl around the church many times, and some carry heavy rocks on their head.

Thousands of people sing "Kulubi songs"

throughout the day. Then the priests come out of the church. In their arms they carry the *Tabot*. This holds the words of the Ten Commandments which were brought to the people by Moses.

The crowds greet it with awe and reverence. The women are especially moved by the presence of the holy Tabot during Kulubi Gabriel. They throw themselves upon the ground to pray. They ululate, or wail loudly, while the Tabot is carried around the church three times. A procession of pilgrims follows it. When this ritual is complete, the Tabot is returned to its place in the holiest part of the church. This marks the end of the festival, and a party mood then takes over the crowds.

The saint answers many pilgrims' prayers. To thank him, they bring food to Kulubi and lay it out on long tables for strangers to eat. They also bring crosses as gifts to the saint. Doves symbolize the Holy Ghost of Christian belief. Saint Gabriel is God's messenger. Religious art in Ethiopia is rich with images of saints and symbols.

25

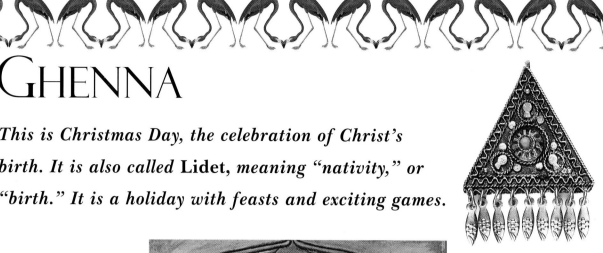

GHENNA

*This is Christmas Day, the celebration of Christ's birth. It is also called **Lidet**, meaning "nativity," or "birth." It is a holiday with feasts and exciting games.*

Ghenna, Ethiopian Christmas, occurs on January 7 or 8. The priests calculate the date each year. These days were first chosen as the celebration of Christ's birth in 1298. The king who ruled at the time chose these days as the official dates.

This is in line with the old Eastern and Orthodox day of celebration. It fits with an old belief that this was the time when the Three Wise Men, or Kings, arrived in Bethlehem to visit the newborn Baby Jesus, lying in a stable.

In the Ethiopian Orthodox Church this holy occasion demands many hours of praying, singing, and elaborate sacred dancing. The church ceremony is an evening-to-dawn affair. The priests are busy.

The people, however, make Ghenna a day to play and enjoy themselves. The women prepare "Christmas breads." These are big, round loaves called *Difo Dabo*. The task of baking Difo Dabo is not a simple one. All the women in the family gather and work hard to produce it, but the shared cooking is often a time to laugh and chatter.

Other items on the Ghenna menu include beef, goat, and lamb. Traditional beers are also a vital part of the holiday meal.

Another traditional part of Ghenna is the *Ghenna Chewata*. It is very similar to hockey. Ghenna Chewata is played on a large open field. Each player holds a long stick, the *dula*, and uses it to knock a wooden ball, the *rur* or *ting*. The goals are two small holes in the ground. The game lasts for hours and demands skill and strength. The young men must be fit to play Chewata.

Still another feature of Ghenna is the game of *Gugs* with riders on horseback. This is a mock battle with charges, evasions, and defenses. Any number of players are involved.

People do attend church sometime during the day, but overall this is a party day.

Much church music was composed by Saint Yared, an Ethiopian musician in the sixth century. Here priests use traditional instruments.

KIRCHA

Food plays a big role at festivals. In the Christian faith the food eaten at Christmas is always different from ordinary, everyday meals. In Ethiopia the wealthy might slaughter a beast to feed their families. Poorer folk, living in one village perhaps or sharing a city street, pool together and buy an ox for the community. The meat is then shared among all the families. This sharing is called *Kircha*. Such largesse with meat is not common in Ethiopia, where oxen are needed to supply milk and to work in the fields.

AN OLD-TIME PAINTING

Before the invention of paper people used to paint and write on vellum, a soft leather made of calf skin. Ethiopian priests still paint on this old material.

We used shammy leather not vellum for this Madonna and Child. They are pictured with African animals instead of the usual stable beasts seen with the Baby Jesus. Copy it or paint your own picture in traditional Ethiopian style.

YOU WILL NEED
Thin wooden board 10" x 6"
Shammy leather 8" x 4"
String
Large needle
All-purpose glue
Tracing paper
Carbon paper
Poster paints

1 Stretch shammy by smoothing and pulling from its center toward its edges. With string and needle catch the shammy with a small stitch. Pull the string across the wood to opposite side from stitch. Stitch again. Repeat this process until shammy lies taut on wood.

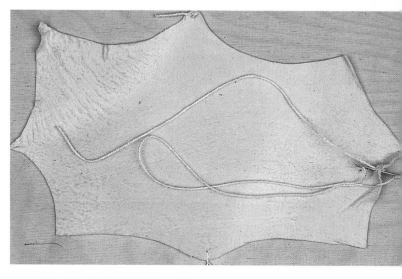

2 Draw your picture on the tracing paper. When you know the size of your image, cover the same size on the shammy with all-purpose glue. Paint it on smoothly. Let it dry.

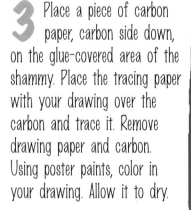

3 Place a piece of carbon paper, carbon side down, on the glue-covered area of the shammy. Place the tracing paper with your drawing over the carbon and trace it. Remove drawing paper and carbon. Using poster paints, color in your drawing. Allow it to dry.

4 To remove from the wooden board, cut the stitched string. Trim the shammy if you wish. The vellum painting can now be framed.

BUHE

*This day, August 19, recalls the Transfiguration of Christ. This is when, after His death, Jesus Christ appeared before three of His followers. The festival is also known as **Debre Tabor**. This may be the old Ethiopian word for Mount Hermon, which is where Christ appeared.*

In Ethiopia *Buhe* is a holiday for the children. Little boys spend days beforehand preparing their *Buhe Jirra,* a whip of braided leather. On Buhe they crack the whip in the air to copy the sound of the sharp voice of God that was heard on Mount Hermon.

Their mothers grind and prepare wheat to make hundreds of little loaves – *mulmul* – that are given to all the children on Buhe day. The boys go from door to door, hoping to receive lots of mulmul. They sing to thank the women who give them loaves.

WORDS TO KNOW

Censer: A container used for burning incense during religious services.

Civil war: A war between citizens of the same country.

Ethiopian Orthodox Church: The Christian church in Ethiopia, which is neither Roman Catholic nor Protestant, but part of the Eastern Orthodox Church.

Eastern Orthodox Church: One of the main branches of Christianity. It consists of a group of national churches found in eastern Europe, the Middle East, and Africa.

Fast: To go without some or all kinds of food and drink deliberately.

Incense: A mixture of gum and spice, often shaped into thin sticks or cones, that gives off a pleasant smell when burned.

Lent: The 40 days between Ash Wednesday and Easter.

Patron saint: A saint who is special to a particular group. Nations, towns, and professions have patron saints.

Pilgrim: A person who makes a religious journey, or pilgrimage, to a holy place.

Relic: A part of the body, clothing, or belongings of Jesus or a saint, preserved as a holy item.

Reliquary: A container in which sacred relics are kept.

Resurrection: The rising of Christ from the dead on Easter Sunday.

Saint: A title given to very holy people by some Christian churches.

Shrine: A place that is sacred to the memory of a holy person, often housing their relics.

Tabot: A tablet or scroll bearing the Ten Commandments.

Ululate: To make high-pitched, wordless wailing sounds.

Vellum: Soft calfskin leather used for painting and writing on.

Votive offering: A gift offered to a god or a saint as a request for help.

ACKNOWLEDGMENTS

WITH THANKS TO:

Yeshi Dimru. Eleanor Lakew. Abebaw Yigzaw. The Staff at St. Gabriel's Shop, London. The Ethiopian Orthodox Church, London.

PHOTOGRAPHY:

All photographs by Bruce Mackie except: John Elliott pp. 11, 15. Cover photograph by Robert Harding Picture Library/David Beatty.

ILLUSTRATIONS BY:

Fiona Saunders pp. 4 – 5. Tracy Rich p. 7. Maps by John Woolford. Afework Mengesha pp. 17, 26, 30. Susan Moxley p. 13 Recipes: Ellen Dupont.

Set Contents